Original title:
The Hickory Harmonies

Copyright © 2025 Creative Arts Management OÜ
All rights reserved.

Author: Ryan Sterling
ISBN HARDBACK: 978-1-80567-221-0
ISBN PAPERBACK: 978-1-80567-520-4

Secrets in the Shadows of Trees

In the shade of the great old oak,
Squirrels plot with quite a joke,
Pinecones drop like secret notes,
As laughter dances on the coats.

A rabbit twirls in a disco groove,
While fireflies glide, trying to prove,
That the best place to prank and tease,
Is beneath those leafy, whispering trees.

The raccoon wears a bandit's mask,
Playing hide and seek is quite the task,
He sneaks and peeks with sneaky skill,
While the owl rolls eyes and swallows its thrill.

Beneath the branches, a party brews,
With acorns clinking in the shoes,
You won't believe what they'll confide,
In the shade, where all secrets hide.

Songs of the Rustling Leaves

Leaves do dance with cheeky glee,
As squirrels sing in harmony.
A gust of wind, they twist and twirl,
Even grumpy owls start to whirl.

Boughs sway low, a limbo call,
The acorns giggle, and then they fall.
The forest floor, a funny sight,
Where critters prance from day to night.

Lullabies in the Twilight Grove

As crickets strum their sleepy tune,
The fireflies light up the moon.
Bunnies hop with sleepy eyes,
While hedgehogs yawn under the skies.

Whispers float on the evening air,
As raccoons play truth or dare.
Their mischief tickles owls awake,
A nighttime laugh is what they make.

Rhythms of the Forest Floor

In the underbrush, a tap tap tap,
Badgers are plotting a great mishap.
Then comes a thump, a stumble, a fall,
Twirling around, they laugh through it all.

The mushrooms giggle, all dressed in spots,
While ants march proudly in wild knots.
Frogs leap high with no sense of shame,
Each one tries to outjump the name!

Ballads of Branch and Bough

Up in the branches, a cat will strum,
Pigeons join in, cooing a hum.
The owls hoot, keeping the beat,
While woodpeckers drum their funny feet.

Raccoons juggle their shiny finds,
Chasing their tails, oh how life binds!
Nature's jesters, clever and spry,
Under the stars, their laughter will fly.

Echoes of the Whispering Trees

In the woods where squirrels play,
Trees gossip in a breezy way.
Branches sway and dance with glee,
Chirping birds join the jubilee.

A raccoon wears a top hat fine,
While ants march in a straightened line.
Laughter echoes through the leaves,
Nature's jest that's sure to please.

A frog croaks jokes from a lily pad,
While bees hum tunes that aren't so bad.
The sun peeks through with a cheeky grin,
As woodland friends dance and spin.

Symphonies Beneath the Canopy

Fiddles played on branches high,
With a fox conducting in the sky.
The owl's hoot's a bass drum thud,
And crickets chirp in rhythmic flood.

A chorus of frogs croaks out the lead,
While ladybugs dance on a tiny steed.
Mice tap dance, and the rabbits cheer,
As nature's band brings joy so near.

An acorn drops, a surprising drum,
And winds whoosh like they're on the run.
Every sound blends in a silly way,
As animals join, come what may.

Melodies of Autumn's Embrace

Leaves rustle with a giggling sound,
Spinning, tumbling, twirling round.
The pumpkins chuckle, what a sight,
In this harvest frolic, pure delight.

Ciders bubbling, sweets do tease,
While squirrels dance among the trees.
The scarecrow laughs, a funny friend,
As autumn's melodies blend and bend.

A turkey struts with a feathered flair,
Winking at the folks who stop and stare.
With every crunch beneath our feet,
The season's humor is hard to beat.

Nature's Stringed Serenade

A woodpecker taps a steady beat,
Strumming sticks with tiny feet.
The breeze hums soft a soothing song,
While lizards dance, the day is long.

A caterpillar plays the lute,
With dangling notes that are quite cute.
The winds swirl in a merry play,
As butterflies twirl without delay.

Waves of laughter fill the glen,
With every note, they start again.
Nature's band in unity,
Sings a serenade, wild and free.

The Poetic Pulse of the Pines

In the woods, where the squirrels dance,
They sneakily nibble on little branches.
With a flick of a tail, they shout, "Not mine!"
While pine cones drop in a funny line.

The chipmunks chatter, they're never shy,
Their tiny voices make everyone sigh.
A raccoon leaps with a wiggle and spin,
And the laughter echoes with every grin.

The owls debate, their wisdom grand,
But they can't find their glasses; they're lost in the sand.
The trees chuckle softly at this silly plight,
As the moonlit sky sparkles with pure delight.

Under the stars, the forest grins wide,
With critters galore in a comical ride.
Nature's a stage full of jest and cheer,
Where the punchlines echo, and the fun is near.

The Enchanted Ground's Echo

Beneath the leaves, where mischief hides,
A gopher pops up, with no place to bide.
"Oh dear!" he squeaks, as he tumbles around,
While the rabbits all laugh at his goofy sound.

A fox, oh so sly, dons boots that are bright,
He struts through the grass, a most curious sight.
The bumblebees buzz, wearing tiny bow ties,
As the daisies giggle at the fox's surprise.

In this merry realm, where the daffodils sway,
Every creature has joined in the fray.
A chorus of chuckles fills the warm air,
With a melody playful, beyond all compare.

As shadows grow long and the sun dips low,
The dance of the critters is all on show.
With joy in their hearts and a skip in their beat,
The echoes of laughter make the night sweet.

Reverberations of the Bark and Bough

The trees tell tales in a wobbly voice,
As squirrels debate, making their choice.
With acorns a-flurry and nuts tossed in glee,
The laughter of branches is wild and free.

A bear in a hat, doing a little jig,
Stomps on the ground with a flutter and dig.
He slips on a banana peel; oh, what a sight!
The other critters roar; it's sheer delight.

A woodpecker drums a whimsical beat,
While the hedgehogs roll in a squeaky retreat.
The laughter of nature rings clear through the air,
As each furry friend jumps without a care.

In the twilight glow, with giggles abound,
The forest unites, joyfully sound.
Here in the woods, where silliness thrives,
The bark and bough sing of merry lives.

The Forager's Melodic Path

On a path through the woods, bright berries abound,
A squirrel waltzes, not making a sound.
He picks up a berry, it pops with a squish,
And suddenly all of his friends make a wish.

A hedgehog arrives with a sack full of snacks,
"Care for a nibble?" he says with a laugh.
But one little taste leads to a grand feast,
Where munching and crunching are surely the least.

The badger plays tunes on an acorn flute,
As everyone dances in a silly suit.
The bumbles form circles, buzzing along,
While nature plays out its joyous song.

With laughter that lingers as shadows grow long,
The path through the woods threads a curious throng.
In this vibrant realm, each tale finds its heart,
Where foraging friends are the best kind of art.

Nature's Woven Melodies

In the woods where owls hoot,
A squirrel dances in a boot.
The tree frogs sing with glee each night,
While fireflies twinkle, oh so bright.

Leaves whisper jokes just out of sight,
A raccoon's antics cause delight.
Bunnies hop in playful pairs,
As chipmunks chuckle on the stairs.

Birds argue over who can fly,
A butterfly waves its wings nearby.
Nature's stage is full of cheer,
With giggles echoing far and near.

So listen close to every sound,
In this funny world, joy is found.
The forest hums a jolly song,
Where laughter lives and all belong.

The Bark's Timeless Tune

On a log, the turtles play,
While otters splash the time away.
A wise old tree leans oh so near,
To share the tales we long to hear.

Squirrels hold a funny race,
While hedgehogs wobble, keep the pace.
The laughter rings through mossy groves,
As critters dance in silly moves.

A bird drops bread from high above,
And groundhogs chuckle, filled with love.
The trunks all creak in rhythmic cheer,
As nature sings, it's clear we're here.

So grab your friends and join the fun,
Under the shining, warming sun.
The bark of laughter fills the air,
With melodies that strip all care.

Whispered Fables in the Breeze

In the meadow, stories flow,
Grasshoppers leap and put on a show.
A caterpillar tells a tale,
Of dreams and hopes on a leafy trail.

Foxes grin with mischief bold,
Sharing secrets the trees have told.
The bees buzz in a rhythmic hive,
As crickets chirp to stay alive.

Each gust of wind brings laughter bright,
Painting the clouds in pure delight.
With whispers soft from flower to tree,
Nature giggles in harmony.

So let's embrace the playful breeze,
In this world of wonders, feel at ease.
As we dance to fables that weave,
In whispers sweet, we do believe.

Chorus of the Evergreen Dream

Amidst the pines, a choir sings,
Of silly frogs and their funny flings.
With every note, a chuckle grows,
As laughter sprouts where sunlight glows.

A bear in shades starts to strut,
While raccoons giggle in their hut.
The critters join with joyful sound,
A feast of fun that's all around.

Trees sway gently, keeping time,
As squirrels stack acorns like a rhyme.
A fox with flair, dashes through,
With mischief bright, he steals the view.

So raise your voice in nature's song,
Where humor lives, and we belong.
In evergreen dreams, let's dance and play,
As laughter lights up every day.

Interludes of the Moonlit Path

Under the moon, the shadows dance,
Critters cavort, seizing the chance.
A raccoon with sparkles on his face,
Sings with a flair, a jolly old grace.

Fireflies blink like stars gone awry,
Buzzing and twirling, oh me, oh my!
A squirrel in starlight finds a new mate,
They twirl and tumble, oh isn't it great?

The crickets chirp, their legs get sore,
Their evening concert is hard to ignore.
With every note, they laugh and sway,
As the moonlight giggles, and joins in the play.

As laughter echoes along the lane,
The night becomes silly, but never a bane.
Each step on the path, brings jolly cheer,
Under a show of the whimsical sphere.

Melodic Embrace of Roots

In the arms of trees, roots have a dance,
Twisting and turning, they take each chance.
With worms as partners, they give it a whirl,
While leaves above giggle, like a playful girl.

The beetles tap-dance, all in a row,
To the rhythm of breezes that gently blow.
Oh, honeybees buzz with laughter profound,
As they join in the melody all around.

Gnarled branches sway, a fine old crew,
With whispers of stories that feel so new.
Each twist of a root brings tales of joy,
In this quirky figure, that nature'll enjoy.

As morning breaks in a bright, funny hue,
The woodland's harmony feels just too true.
With giggles resounding, and chuckles from trees,
In this melodic embrace, there's more fun, if you please!

The Melody of Shaded Life

Under the leaves, where shadows play,
Squirrels commune in a comic ballet.
A rabbit hops lightly, in shoes too big,
While a warbler trills, doing a jig.

The ferns sway slowly, like they're in bliss,
With whispers of secrets that none can miss.
A lazy old tortoise joins in the spree,
As the sunbeam flickers, oh what glee!

Ants march in lines, with hats all askew,
Carrying crumbs like a funny crew.
They chuckle and stumble, what a delight,
In the shade of the trees, life feels just right.

Amidst the dance of the greenery lush,
A symphony brews, with a vibrant hush.
Every moment's a jest, in nature's grand show,
This melody's bright, as the heartbeats flow.

Rhapsody of the Thicket's Heart

In the thicket's heart, where mischief thrives,
Creatures put on their funny high-fives.
A fox in a hat, with an elegant air,
Twists and turns with a wiggle and flair.

The hedgehogs giggle, rolling in heaps,
While owls, with glasses, gossip and peep.
Laughter erupts, like bubbles of soda,
As hedges join in, what a fine quota!

With each rustle and squeak, the night grows bright,
As friendships are forged, oh what a sight!
Amidst all this fun, they bound and explore,
In the rhapsody, they will always want more.

From dusk till dawn, the antics unfold,
With warm-hearted jests, and stories retold.
In thickets of laughter, they find their true art,
Celebrating life, in the thicket's grand heart.

The Woodland Whimsy

In a forest of laughter, trees sway with glee,
Squirrels in tuxedos sip acorns for tea.
Frogs in bow ties croak tunes most absurd,
While raccoons dance wildly, tails flipping, not blurred.

A squirrel juggles nuts, what a silly sight,
While chipmunks do pirouettes, bringing delight.
Leaves clap their hands to the beat of the show,
As deer stomp their hooves to the rhythm, aglow.

A hedgehog with rhythm taps rocks like a pro,
While owls cheer and hoot, putting on quite a show.
Even the starlight can't help but smile,
As critters join in the fun, mile after mile.

With giggles and laughter, the woodlands alive,
In this whimsical jam where the creatures can thrive.
Each branch holds a story, each twig sings a song,
Where nature's a stage, and we all just belong.

Lullaby of the Leafy Lattice

Under a quilt of leaves, whispers loom,
Bunnies in pajamas make every room.
Shadows weave stories in the soft, golden light,
While crickets compose tunes that last through the night.

Fireflies sway gently, like dancers of grace,
In the hush of the evening, they light up the place.
A raccoon in slippers spills juice on the floor,
As all of his friends laugh and beg him for more.

A slumbering fox snuggles close to a stone,
Dreaming of adventures, yet never alone.
Each rustle and giggle brings comfort and cheer,
As night wraps them softly, the woodland draws near.

With lullabies humming beneath starry skies,
Nature holds secrets, where silliness lies.
In whispers of breezes, the night sings a tune,
While laughter embraces the silver-lit moon.

The Chorus of the Quiet Canopy

Beneath a vast canopy, whispers collide,
Where trees stitch the sky, and owls take pride.
A band of young critters tune up their cheers,
As laughter and joy float through wagging ears.

Squirrels play fiddles, with nuts as their bows,
Bunnies tap dance, in their soft, fluffy clothes.
A raccoon strums leaves, like a harp on a stream,
While turtles with microphoned shells softly beam.

This lyrical forest, where mischief takes flight,
Sings songs of the silly, from morning to night.
Each critter contributes to a melody sweet,
Creating a symphony where joy and fun meet.

Together they harmonize, laughter their guide,
In playful duet, they dance side by side.
With each twinkle of stars, and each leafy embrace,
The chorus of canopies embraces this space.

Rhymes of the Rooted Realm

In the rooted realm where the oddballs reside,
Twirling and spinning, the critters confide.
With acorns for maracas, they join in the fun,
Each twig and each leaf, a dance just begun.

A hedgehog recites with a snicker and grin,
While rabbits breakdance on a soft bed of skin.
The whispers of fauna combine into words,
As nature composes, amusing like birds.

Chasing the shadows, they leap and they bound,
Each root holds a secret, a giggle unbound.
With laughter like raindrops, they splash and they play,
In the rhythm of roots, they frolic and sway.

So gather 'round, friends, in this playful parade,
Where every tiptoe sends joy on cascade.
In a world full of whimsy, they frolic and scream,
These rhymes of the rooted realm are the dream.

Ballad of the Overhanging Bough

Beneath the branches, squirrels meet,
Swapping tales of nimble feet.
One lost his acorn, and oh what a fuss,
Now it's a quest, they laugh and they fuss.

A bird drops by, in a comical fight,
With a shadowy worm, what a funny sight!
Worm wiggles away, high tailed and swift,
Birdy's got nothing, no wormy gift.

An owl in the night, with a booming hoot,
Claims he's the king in his snazzy suit.
But all of us giggle, we know what he lacks,
It's wisdom, not clothes, that fills in the cracks.

So gather 'round roots, share a chuckle or two,
Life in the boughs is a whimsical view.
With laughs in the leaves and joy in the air,
We'll dance in the moonlight, without a care.

Chorus of the Chirping Crickets

Crickets compose their night-time song,
A symphony of chirps, all night long.
They gather in droves, on blades of green,
Their little legs tapping, a lively scene.

One cricket boasts, 'I'm the best of the band!'
While another makes music without a hand.
But the louder they chirp, the more it confuses,
What's music to them might just be bad blueses.

They practice their notes under the starlit skies,
With dreams of fame, and all of their ties.
Yet when dawn emerges, their giggles unfold,
Turning cease and desist into stories retold.

So join their wild choir, just take a stance,
Together with crickets, we'll all join the dance.
No need for a stage, just grass and some night,
In harmony we'll gather, 'til morning's first light.

Twilight in the Timberland

Twilight falls gently, the shadows play,
As chipmunks hold court, with tales to relay.
One claims to have seen a majestic stag,
While others just giggle, and snicker and brag.

Fireflies flicker, like tiny bright stars,
Chasing each other, oh how quick they are!
One bumps a tree, made quite the display,
Fell on the cat who had come out to play.

A raccoon named Marvin thinks he's the boss,
Wearing a hat made from something he tossed.
He struts through the twilight, with laughter galore,
Till he trips on a root, and tumbles, oh what a roar!

So evenings in woods bring laughter anew,
With critters so silly, and antics so true.
Just listen and watch, as the forest goes wild,
Every critter's a comedian, every last child.

Notes from the Nature's Nook

In a nook of the woods, where the wild things play,
A deer tells a joke in a funny, sweet way.
'The grass is so green, it's a feast, what a treat!
But my friend the cow won't share any meat!'

Nearby a rabbit hops, with a spring in his step,
Juggling some carrots, a comedic rep.
He trips on a root, makes quite a scene,
With laughter erupting, he's still on the green.

A bear rolls around, with a fumble and flip,
Chasing after berries as they take a dip.
He wipes off the mess with a chuckle so wide,
Says, 'I'm just keeping my midnight snacks fried!'

So take a moment, in nature's delight,
To chuckle at critters and bask in their light.
These silly antics, under sun and the moon,
Fill our hearts with laughter, it's nature's sweet tune.

Verses of the Leafy Canopy

In the branches, squirrels dance,
Chasing shadows, in a prance.
Nuts are tossed with gleeful cheer,
Watch your head, or they'll come near!

The leaves whisper secrets, quite absurd,
They gossip about that cheeky bird.
With acorns as jewels, they strut and sway,
Making mischief all day, hooray!

A raccoon plays the piano with flair,
While owls hoot, pretending to care.
Foxes giggle in their cozy lair,
Nature's jesters, without a care!

But when the sun sets, they all must hide,
In their leafy homes, no need to bide.
They dream of nuts and acorn pies,
And tomorrow's fun under the skies!

An Anthem for the Woods

In the woods, where laughter rings,
Frogs wear crowns, and sing their flings.
Beetles march, a little parade,
To celebrate the fun they've made.

Twilight dances on the brook,
Here comes a deer with quite the look.
Wearing a scarf made of moss and lace,
Turning heads in this woodland race!

Mice in tuxedos, sipping tea,
Chattering 'bout the latest spree.
A chipmunk with a top hat, oh so neat,
Invites them all to his grand feast!

Each tree sways to the joyful tune,
Beneath the sparkle of the moon.
As the night wraps all snug and tight,
The woods echo with laughter, pure delight!

Songs of the Sylvan Realm

A playful breeze tickles the trees,
While bunnies hop with utmost ease.
Their floppy ears bounce to the beat,
Of a melody oh so sweet!

Owls wear glasses to read the news,
About the antics of forest crews.
Squirrels debate on the best tree,
In a contest of who's nuttiest, you see!

Raccoons wear masks, villains they claim,
Stealing snacks is their favorite game.
They laugh and cheer through the night,
Till dawn comes with its golden light.

The trees join in with a creaky song,
Swaying gently, where all belong.
A symphony of critters, wild and free,
In the woodland orchestra, joyful glee!

Harmonious Echoes of Time

Amidst the pines, they chirp and chat,
With ruffled feathers, oh, how they spat!
The wisdom of the owl, or so they say,
But his jokes always lead them astray.

The chipmunks gather for their big show,
With tiny instruments, all in tow.
A dance breaks out, right on the spot,
With twirls and hops, oh, what a lot!

The sun tumbles down, painting the sky,
As fireflies flicker and start to fly.
They form a chorus, bright little lights,
Guiding the moon through whimsical nights.

In this enchanted dome of glee,
Nature sings in harmony.
Every rustle, every chime,
Echoing laughter through space and time!

The Musical Dance of the Earth

Beneath the sun, the worms do sway,
They groove to beats in their own way.
A snail in shades, with swagger bold,
Claims he's a star, or so I'm told.

The grasshoppers jump, a lively crew,
With banjos strung from morning dew.
The frogs croak tunes, a croaky choir,
Singing songs that never tire.

Ants march in line, a marching band,
Each one holds a crumb, oh so grand!
Dancing in formation, they twirl and spin,
For every crumb, they all win!

All around, the laughter flows,
As nature's band steals the show.
A symphony, wild, with no refrain,
Where every twist brings joyful rain.

Cadence Among the Leaves

The leaves they rustle, breaking news,
In whispers soft, with tiny snooze.
A squirrel jigs, with nuts held tight,
He laughs at all who dance at night.

Breezes hum through branches tall,
A chorus where the critters call.
A raccoon winks, in moonlight's beam,
He's planning tricks, a naughty dream.

The pine trees sway, with trunks so grand,
Wobbling legs, do you understand?
Their needles tap like little feet,
In rhythm loud, a forest beat.

With acorns dropping, a plucky beat,
Nature's jam holds no defeat.
In every shout, and every cheer,
The cadence calls, come join us here!

Melodies of the Majestic Oak

An oak tree stands, so wise and proud,
He's the king of trees, draws quite a crowd.
With arms outstretched, he talks so bright,
To every bird that takes to flight.

His branches sway, a dance divine,
With leaf-shaped friends in perfect line.
Owls hoot low, with echoes clear,
Proudly proclaiming, "We live here!"

Beneath the shade, the critters croon,
Making melodies beneath the moon.
A dancing beetle, full of zest,
Says, "Join my jam! It's simply the best!"

The oak replies with creaks and groans,
His roots tap softly on ancient stones.
Together they form a merry song,
In this kingdom where we all belong.

The Secret Chords of the Silent Grove

In a grove where whispers play,
Secrets dance and twirl away.
A fox in shoes, oh so divine,
Struts his stuff, says, "Isn't it fine?"

The shadows sway, they chuckle low,
As fireflies put on quite a show.
A raccoon steals a silly glance,
Joining in on nature's dance.

With hidden chords, the trees intone,
Melodies from woods unknown.
Grass blades hum beneath the feet,
A funny tune, a rhythmic beat.

The frogs in hats do pirouette,
In harmony, they won't forget.
When dusk descends, and stars take flight,
The grove erupts with pure delight.

Sylvan Echoes at Dusk

Underneath the twilight's glow,
The owls exchange some witty woe,
Squirrels dance in a leafy jig,
While raccoons plot their heisty gig.

A deer joins in with quite the flair,
Twirling 'round without a care,
Frogs croak out a grand old tune,
As crickets snap beneath the moon.

Mice hold court 'neath the old oak,
Telling tales with laughter's yoke,
A fox comes by, quite sly and spry,
Tripping over his well-worn tie.

The curtain falls on this delight,
As stars begin their playful flight,
Nature's laugh fills the night air,
In echoes of their merry flair.

Melodies among the Branches

In the trees, the music swells,
As chipmunks brag and hoot like bells,
A bear hums softly, quite offbeat,
While bees buzz dance with happy feet.

Frogs are crooning in the reeds,
With notes as high as willow seeds,
A parrot squawks, 'It's karaoke!'
While crickets chirp, 'We are no smokey!'

Beneath the boughs, a picnic spread,
With sandwiches on crusts of bread,
The laughter floats like butterflies,
As raccoons gasp at silly skies.

From branch to branch, a comical chase,
As feathers fly in a madcap race,
The woods resound with giggles and glee,
It's a wild show for all to see.

Nature's Gentle Serenade

Morning breaks in playful tones,
As frogs and squirrels crack their bones,
A woodpecker knocks on a tree,
'Is anyone home? I'd like some tea!'

The sunbeams dance on rivulets,
While chipmunks twirl in fancy sets,
A butterfly flirts with a flower,
Unfazed by bees in their buzzing power.

Tall grasses sway with laughter bright,
As daisies giggle through the night,
A hedgehog rolls with joyful glee,
While ants march on, a comedy spree.

As twilight drapes its gentle cloak,
The moon erupts with a silly joke,
In harmony, the forest sings,
Of nature's fun and whimsical things.

The Lullaby of Ancient Roots

Beneath old roots, the stories creep,
As shadows whisper, giggling deep,
A turtle hums a sleepy rhyme,
While fireflies blink in perfect time.

Ancient trees sway with a grin,
Recalling tales where tales begin,
A raccoon twirls in puppet show,
As pine needles fall like hushes slow.

Owl jokes land with a cushy thud,
As stars applaud from above, so stud,
With nature's lull, they drift away,
To dream of mischief come next day.

Sounds of slumber, a cozy spree,
In forests deep with laughter free,
Where roots conspire with branches grand,
To weave a tale across the land.

The Lilt of Nature's Breath

Beneath the branches, birds do jest,
Their tweets like laughter, never rest.
Squirrels chatter, in their little dance,
Chasing shadows, a furry romance.

A breeze will giggle, as it sweeps by,
Rustling leaves that seem to sigh.
Nature's chorus, a merry parade,
With every note, the world's charade.

Bumbling bees in pollen-gold,
Their wobbly flight, a sight so bold.
Frogs croak jokes on lily's throne,
Under the moon, they're never alone.

And when the sun yawns, the night takes cue,
Crickets hum tunes, like they always do.
In the forest dance, they share a joke,
In this leafy realm where laughter's bespoke.

Treetop Tales in Twilight

As shadows stretch and day takes flight,
The owls hoot tales that spark delight.
Bats flap by like tiny kites,
In the fading glow, they fuel their flights.

Squirrels whisper secrets, cheeky and sly,
About hidden nuts and the great pie in the sky.
Frogs congregate, a croaking crew,
Their ribbeting echoes, an evening cue.

Fireflies flicker as if they play,
In a glowing dance for the end of the day.
Each blink is a giggle, a glint in the dark,
Nature's own spark to light up the park.

In the stillness, creatures share a laugh,
A moose trips over a misplaced path.
Under the stars, their chuckles resound,
In treetop tales, pure joy can be found.

Whispers of the Old Grove

In the old grove, trees gossip and sway,
Squirrels enact a comical play.
With tiny acorns, they plot and scheme,
As if the forest were their grand dream.

The wind, a joker, tosses the leaves,
Crafting pranks that no one believes.
Chipmunks giggle in perfect sync,
Their chubby cheeks full of playful drink.

Mice in the maize, they dance with flair,
Wearing tiny shoes with whimsical care.
When the moon grins, shadows take flight,
Heartbeat of mischief in the gathering night.

As laughter erupts from the oak and the pine,
The old grove hums, feeling just fine.
With every whisper, joy flows like wine,
Nature's own jesters, a humorous line.

Ballad of the Rustic Breeze

Oh, the rustic breeze knows how to tease,
It stirs up laughter with the utmost ease.
Sending leaves twirling, a whimsical show,
Participating in dance, as if in the know.

A chipmunk struts, proud of its stash,
While a crow caws loudly, creating a clash.
Crickets serenade under twilight's glow,
In this picnic of joy, everyone's a pro.

The flowers gossip, their petals unfurl,
Spreading sweet scents in a colorful swirl.
Bluebirds chime in, with a fluttery cheer,
Crafting a ballad that all love to hear.

As stars twinkle brightly, a backdrop divine,
The rustic breeze hums, a melody fine.
In this joyous concert, nature's the bard,
With every note, maturity's marred.

Rhapsody of the Rustling Grass

In a meadow where the daisies dance,
The grass whispers secrets, given a chance.
A squirrel in a tuxedo, with a top hat high,
Twirls on a log, oh my, oh my!

The breeze joins in with a giggling sigh,
As petals join the party, fluttering high.
With ants doing cha-cha under the sun,
This grassland soirée is just so much fun!

Sounds of laughter echo in the air,
While bees buzz off to a sweet lover's lair.
A rabbit in shades, oh so smooth,
Taps to the rhythm, making his move!

As twilight descends, they all start to rest,
Underneath the starry blanket they nest.
But the crickets are crooning, a jazzy delight,
With the grass as their stage, oh what a night!

Notes from the Nesting Birds

In the high branches where feathers flutter,
Birds gather for a meeting, no room for clutter.
A cardinal cracks jokes, making them squawk,
While a wise old owl gives a sleepy talk.

A robin rolls by with a wormy treat,
Says, 'It's a gourmet meal, can't be beat!'
Chirps turn to laughter as they share their tales,
Of daring flights and how to dodge the gales.

Finches in flappers dance in a line,
With a catchy tune that's simply divine.
All is merry in their treetop flat,
Until a loud crow steals the hat!

They plot a revenge, but it's all in jest,
For friendship is key, and they're truly blessed.
With music and laughter, they sing till dark,
Their happy notes echo, leaving a mark.

The Symphony of Twilight Twigs

As the sun dips low and shadows grow long,
Twilight twigs chirp in a leafy song.
A raccoon wearing glasses hums a tune,
While fireflies flash like stars in June.

Woodpeckers tap out a clever beat,
Creating a rhythm that's truly sweet.
While a toad in a top coat leaps with glee,
Declaring, 'I'm the prince of this jamboree!'

Crickets join in, their voices bright,
Casting spells of laughter into the night.
A bat takes a bow, flapping with grace,
As frogs croak the chorus, filling the space.

The moon winks down, joining the fun,
With beams of silver that dance and run.
In this whimsical world where twig meets bark,
Every creature knows how to make their mark!

Echoes of the Enchanted Glade

In a glade where the daisies twinkle and sway,
Frogs in tuxedos come out to play.
A fox tells tales that twist and turn,
While owls hoot in laughter, their eyes all aglow, they learn.

The trees wiggle their branches in time to the beat,
As a hedgehog in goggles dances on his feet.
Laughter and giggles ripple through the air,
Creatures all joined in this magical fair.

A squirrel busts moves on a twiggy dance floor,
While a porcupine plays the piano encore.
Every critter chimes in with their own silly groove,
Creating a harmony that makes their hearts move.

When the sun sets low, and the stars come aglow,
The glade whispers secrets only they know.
So under the moon, they sway and sing,
Spreading joy through the night, what happiness brings!

The Trilling of the Tranquil Trees

In the forest, the trees start to hum,
Squirrels tap dance, oh, what fun!
With a breeze that tickles the leaves,
Their laughter flows like honeyed eves.

Birds chirp tales of ancient lore,
While raccoons play poker by the door.
Branches sway to the silly beat,
As the bees get up and tap their feet.

Sunlight plays with shadows so grand,
And the grass joins in, taking a stand.
The critters waltz, twirl in delight,
While the trees shake off their bark in flight.

So come and join this playful waltz,
For the forest holds no faults.
Just laughter and songs on every breeze,
In the trilling of the tranquil trees.

Notes of the Nostalgic Nook

In a corner of the woods so snug,
Lies a bench that fits like a drug.
The owls roll their eyes at the jokes,
While the flowers giggle at all the folks.

A chipmunk recites his favorite rhyme,
A turtle taps, keeping perfect time.
Old memories dance like fireflies,
As laughter swirls through the autumn skies.

The breeze croons soft, a gentle tease,
Telling secrets among the trees.
With notes of the past in every glance,
Nature invites us all to dance.

Grab your hat, let's take a stroll,
In this nook, let's lose control.
For laughter rings through time's soft nook,
In the harmonies we forsook.

Chorus of the Crescendoing Canopies

Up in the branches, a concert starts,
With acorns drumming and leafy hearts.
The winds blow smooth, strumming the air,
While the sun beams down with a cheeky flare.

Fluttering birds join in the song,
Chirping out rhythms, oh so strong.
The squirrels add giggles, soft and sweet,
Making this chorus a wondrous treat.

Every rustle tells a quirky tale,
As critters laugh without fail.
The trees sway, lost in the fun,
While leaves dance round, their twirl just begun.

So gather near, don't miss this show,
Where nature's rhythms put on a glow.
In every note, find joy and peace,
In the chorus that will never cease.

The Timeless Tune of Trunks and Twigs

Beneath the canopy, shadows play,
While squirrels dance the day away.
Their chittering fills the vibrant air,
Making even grumpy trees care.

Twigs tap along to an unseen beat,
As ants march on, so tiny and neat.
With each trunk's twist, a new joke unfolds,
In nature's realm, where laughter holds.

The brook sings softly, a gentle croon,
While frogs add to it, a quirky tune.
The leaves giggle when the breezes tease,
Creating symphonies with the greatest ease.

So come, dear friend, and lend an ear,
To the melodies that bring us cheer.
In trunks and twigs, find joy and glee,
With the timeless tunes from the land of free.

The Dance of the Leafy Shadows

In the garden where the shadows play,
Leaves do a jig at the end of day.
Squirrels twirl, and acorns bounce,
While birds compete for the best of pounce.

The sun dips low, but the fun won't cease,
A frog croaks loudly, in blissful peace.
Butterflies join with a graceful bend,
It's a leafy party that has no end.

Laughter rings out from the whispering trees,
As chipmunks dance to the lightest breeze.
A rabbit hops, with a flick of its tail,
Creating a scene that makes hearts sail.

So join the dance with your very best twirl,
In nature's amphitheater, let joy unfurl.
With shadows laughing in each little nook,
Join the leafy dance, come take a look!

Harmonies of the Wind-Kissed Trees

Whispers of woodlands, hear the trees talk,
Bantering breezes on an old mossy rock.
Branches chuckle, with each little sway,
As leaves rustle secrets in a playful way.

A crow on a branch starts a raucous tune,
While nature's chorus hums under the moon.
The owls give hoots, adding humor to night,
With echoes of laughter, oh, what a sight!

Beneath the canopy, critters convene,
With ants telling tales of the great unseen.
The fox, with a grin, shares riddles galore,
In the woodland theater, they always want more.

So listen up close, the trees sing out loud,
With harmonies woven, make nature so proud.
Join in the fun, let your spirits be free,
In this whimsical world of the wind-kissed trees!

Murmurs of the Maple Mist

In the soft light of the groggy dawn,
Maple leaves whisper, as night is withdrawn.
With giggles of dew, they shimmer and sway,
Inviting the sun for a delightful ballet.

A raccoon scales branches, with mischief galore,
While squirrels toss acorns, a playful uproar.
Fog rolls in gently, a soft cotton sheet,
Wrapping the forest in a snug, whimsical greet.

The creek chuckles on, with a splash and a glee,
As frogs croak their charm, oh, what harmony!
Twirl with the mist, let your laughter unbind,
In this playful realm, joy's not hard to find.

So meander through whispers, let your heart stay light,
In maple mist mornings, everything feels right.
Join the frolic, let your worries drift,
In the gentle embrace of nature's gift!

Chords of the Woodland Heart

In the heart of the woods, a tune comes alive,
With chirping and chattering, all creatures thrive.
The woodpecker drums, keeping beat with the breeze,
While rabbits hop along, swaying through trees.

A band of raccoons put on quite the show,
With antics so silly, they steal the tableau.
The skunk strikes a pose, all dressed in black and white,
As the forest laughs softly at this charming sight.

Underneath the stars, they've gathered to sing,
Echoing softly, the joy of the spring.
A coyote howls, adding flair to the night,
While fireflies dance, casting a magical light.

In woodland rhythms, let giggles run free,
As the heart of this forest keeps time with glee.
Join the celebration, oh, let laughter impart,
In the vibrant symphony of the woodland heart!

The Gentle Strum of the Ferns

In the glade where laughter grows,
Frogs croak tunes nobody knows.
Dance with the leaves, sway with the breeze,
Tickling the air, it's sure to please.

A squirrel plays on a tiny lute,
While daisies laugh in their bright little suit.
The sun winks down with a golden grin,
As critters gather, let the jests begin!

Worms tap dance, the mushrooms cheer,
Each note sung makes the flowers leer.
Oh, what a sight, oh, what a sound,
In this woodland fun, joy's unbound!

So strum along, let your heart be light,
The ferns jig and twirl in pure delight.
With each silly note that floats on by,
Nature's giggles fill the sky.

Whispers of the Wandering Wind

The gusty chuckles weave through trees,
Tickling the branches, shaking the leaves.
"Do you hear that?" asks a curious bee,
"It's the breeze playing hide-and-seek with me!"

The wind whooshes past, a playful prank,
Pushing a dandelion, oh how it sang!
It tugs at the hats, it pulls at the hair,
Spreading giggles everywhere!

Clouds roll in, wearing silly hats,
While raindrops tumble like playful cats.
Each splash is a joke that brightens the gloom,
Nature's stand-up in a vibrant costume!

So listen close to that playful hum,
A funny tale that's sure to come.
Join in the laughter, follow the call,
In the dance of the wind, we're all in thrall.

A Folk Song for the Flora

Petals in pink start to sway,
Singing soft tunes in a floral ballet.
"Let's have a picnic!" the daisies shout,
While lilies laugh, twirling about.

The bumblebees buzz with a funny sting,
Making the blossoms wear their bling.
With each sticky sip, they share a grin,
Nature's laughter echoes from within.

Sunflowers stretch to catch the notes,
Their golden heads in jolly coats.
As crickets chirp in sweet duet,
Every line's another laugh we get!

Join in the fun, let your heart be light,
As petals giggle in sheer delight.
With every note, the colors bloom,
In the symphony that chases gloom.

Sopranos of the Solitary Shrubs

Among the thickets, a voice so sweet,
A shrub sings low, tapping its feet.
"I'm the tallest, can't you see?"
While bushes nod in a lively spree!

The sparrows join in, a merry band,
Singing tunes across the land.
With every chirp, and every cheer,
A comedy show, oh, come and hear!

Thorns make faces, sharp and proud,
As flowers giggle, forming a crowd.
Whispers of laughter rustle the leaves,
In this shrubbery concert, humor weaves.

So gather round, let the jokes abound,
With each silly laugh, we're spellbound.
Sing with the shrubs, in nature's choir,
In the laughter of flora, hearts never tire.

Serenade of the Swaying Sycamores

In the breeze the branches dance,
With squirrels stealing a glance.
They twirl and sway with such delight,
While crickets chirp into the night.

A bird drops a twig on a frog,
Who jumps and croaks, creating a fog.
The leaves chuckle at this ruckus,
As laughter rings within the dusk.

A raccoon sneaks in for a snack,
While rabbits play a game, no lack.
The moon beams down on this delight,
As shadows waltz, they take to flight.

Oh, let them sway, those trees so grand,
With their antics, they take a stand.
Nature's troop, a comical sight,
In the serenade of pure delight.

The Hum of the Hidden Hollow

In the hollow, there's a hum,
Of bees that dance and drums that thrum.
The owls hoot out a silly tune,
As shadows sway beneath the moon.

A snake slips past on tiptoe tight,
While frogs compete in croaky fright.
The bumblebees buzz round the bloom,
Joining in on the buzzing boom.

A family of skunks leaps in line,
Twirling, swirling, oh how they shine!
Their tails raised up, a sight so grand,
In hidden antics they take their stand.

The trees sway gently, their leaves applaud,
For the vibrant fun in this hidden façade.
In the echo of laughter, secrets dwell,
As nature hums her own lively spell.

Hymn of the Harmonious Hearth

By the fire, the critters cheer,
With a flick and a spark, they gather near.
The raccoon juggles with sticks of pine,
While the rabbit snickers at the design.

A family of deer, with tinsel on head,
Join the party, oh what a spread!
They nibble on snacks, share stories bold,
As the tales of the forest unfold.

A bear joins in, he rolls on the ground,
With laughter and joy, what a merry sound!
S'mores made with acorns, a tasty sight,
As fireflies dance in the warm twilight.

The night wears on, with fun galore,
In the heart of the woods, there's always more.
With every giggle, the love they share,
In the hymn of the hearth, they breathe the air.

Nature's Conversational Cadence

In the park, a chatter prevails,
With whispered secrets in the trails.
A squirrel in debate with a crow,
Over acorns, their opinions flow.

The wind joins in, a gusty sigh,
As butterflies flit and passersby.
They gossip of flowers, scents, and sights,
In a symphony of nature's delights.

A turtle slow, with wisdom profound,
Shares tales of the land, just hanging 'round.
The frogs croak back with loud retorts,
A lively exchange in their little courts.

With every rustle, a tale unfolds,
In this grand stage, laughter beholds.
Nature converses, both witty and warm,
Creating a cadence, a joyful charm.

Reverberations in the Old Oak

In the old oak's branches, a squirrel does dance,
He twirls and he leaps, does a silly prance.
With acorns aplenty, he shakes all around,
Causing giggles from friends, such silly sounds.

The woodpecker drums, it's a clumsy affair,
Knocking on bark with a feathery flair.
As bugs start to buzz, they form a loud crowd,
The tree shakes with laughter, it's boisterous, proud.

Branches sway gently, like dancers in line,
Whispering secrets, sharing tales over wine.
Juicy fruit dangles, ripe hopes on display,
Each bite is a laugh in the sun's warm ray.

When winds blow a tune, the leaves rustle play,
Nature's orchestra joins, a concert at bay.
In this old oak's heart, the fun never stops,
With rhythms and laughter, it's music that pops.

Notes from the Sunlit Glade

In a sun-kissed glade where the daisies gleam,
A rabbit jumps high, how absurd it must seem!
Chasing its tail, it spins round with delight,
While frogs croak in chorus, a comical sight.

The butterflies flutter, all colors and flair,
They giggle at bumbles that tumble mid-air.
A chipmunk nearby, with a nut in its paws,
Cracks jokes with the crickets, 'What's got four legs and flaws?'

Under rays of the sun in this merry old patch,
Laughter and frolic like souls come to hatch.
Each rustle of leaves, every chirp a refrain,
In this glade of laughter, joy flows like rain.

As evening descends, with a wink and a grin,
The moon joins the fun, it's a party to win.
The stars twinkle bright, like a wink from above,
In the sunlit glade, it's laughter we love.

The Tree's Secret Sonata

In the still of the night, the branches take flight,
Whispers of secrets in the moon's silver light.
A raccoon in shadows, strums on a string,
A mischievous tune, the tree starts to sing.

Swaying with grace, the leaves tap their toes,
As shadows play games where the wild river flows.
The owl hoots a beat, a wise old fellow,
With quirks in his dance, he's quite the silly yellow.

Breezes hum softly, making music out loud,
While fireflies twinkle, form a luminous crowd.
Each flicker, a note that dances in air,
Creating a symphony, without a care.

In this secret sonata, the night is alive,
With critters and tunes, oh how they all thrive!
A vibrant ensemble, in nature's embrace,
The tree's secret song, a hilarious space.

A Symphony of Shelter and Shade

Beneath leafy canopies, the laughter is bold,
A picnic of joy wrapped in stories retold.
The ants march in line, like a parade on the ground,
While bees sing a buzz that's hilariously loud.

Tangled in laughter, the best friends convene,
With sandwiches glowing, a comical scene.
A raccoon steals fries, what a mischievous thief!
"Don't mind me!" he chuckles, "This is my belief!"

The sun peeks through branches, with a wink in its shine,
While shadows do jive, keeping time with the line.
The breeze brings the chuckles, as leaves join the fun,
In this symphony of shade, where laughter is spun.

As day turns to dusk, the tones softly blend,
Nature giggles along, it's a song without end.
With each note a giggle, in this lively array,
A symphony crafted, in shelter and play.

Melodic Footsteps on Forest Floors

In the woods, we dance so bright,
With squirrels joining, what a sight!
Feet tapping to a playful beat,
Rabbits bounce and join our heat.

Branches sway in silly glee,
A raccoon sings in harmony.
Leaves rustle like a ticklish tease,
Nature giggles in the breeze.

Oh, the trees can't help but sway,
As we laugh the day away.
With each stomp upon the ground,
Our joyful tunes are all around.

Beneath the sky, so wide and blue,
Footsteps lead the merry crew.
With every hop and every spin,
The forest finds its rhythm within.

The Essence of the Evergreen Echo

In evergreens, a voice does rise,
Echoing between the skies.
A silly tune the pine trees hum,
While hedgehogs laugh, oh what fun!

Mossy beds where giggles lie,
Chipmunks wink with a boisterous sigh.
Each echo cracks up the ground,
As laughter spins all 'round and 'round.

Can you hear the frogs croon low?
With every ribbit, they steal the show.
Nature's chorus, loud and free,
Each note dances like a bee.

So join the song that nature's made,
In this silly, leafy parade.
With every whisper of the breeze,
The echoes burst with chuckles and ease.

Whispered Wishes Beneath the Trees

Underneath the oak so grand,
We craft wishes with our hand.
Squirrels scurry with a grin,
As we share our dreams within.

Whispers float like cotton fluff,
"More acorns, please!" we laugh, "Enough!"
Every trunk has secrets wide,
Nature chuckles, can't decide.

With every wish, the grass sways too,
A tiny mouse joins our crew.
Dreams swirl up through leafy lanes,
Brightening up the forest plains.

So let your laughter take a flight,
Beneath the boughs, it feels so right.
As wishes twirl like butterflies,
The trees lean in to hear our sighs.

The Resounding Harmony of Roots

The roots beneath start to laugh,
As they feel our joyful path.
Twisting, turning, in a dance,
Every bump gives joy a chance.

Feisty fungi cheer us on,
While butterflies just swoon and yawn.
The ground shakes with giggles mild,
For even rock is nature's child.

As roots embrace the silly games,
The forest knows our playful names.
When we stomp, the whole world sings,
Highlighting all the joy it brings.

So join the fun beneath the earth,
Every twist reveals new mirth.
With laughter woven into the soil,
The resounding joy makes hearts uncoil.

Hymn of the Tree Trunks

Oh, the trunks stand tall, quite a sight,
The squirrels chat loud, taking flight.
They giggle and chuckle, just ain't right,
In this woodlands party, hearts feel light.

Beneath leafy crowns, the shadows play,
Tree trunks nodding, come what may.
With acorn hats, and pranks in sway,
Share a laugh as night turns to day.

Their bark tells tales, quirky and grand,
Of chipmunks in jammies, oh, so unplanned.
A raccoon in shades, strumming a band,
In this silly choir, laughter is fanned.

So join in the joy, let your spirit sway,
With nature's jesters, let's dance and play.
In the midst of barks, come laugh and stay,
In the hymn of the trunks, all worries decay.

Whispers in the Willow's Dance

The willows sway, a gentle tease,
Their branches whisper secrets with ease.
A raccoon twirls, with a flair that frees,
While the frogs croon songs like buzzing bees.

A dance of shadows, they prance and glide,
With every breeze, the giggles collide.
The moon winks down, it cannot hide,
At this silly party, joy is applied.

The bushes burst forth with laughter loud,
As fireflies blink, forming a crowd.
With each little hop, they feel so proud,
In willow's embrace, mischief is plowed.

So sway with the willows, in this merry trance,
Let the night tickle you, give joy a chance.
It's a whimsical world where dreamers prance,
In the whispers of trees, join the dance.

The Forest's Silent Song

In the forest deep, where shadows cheer,
A bunny's giggle rings oh-so-clear.
With a wiggle and bounce, it draws us near,
In this silent song, there's nothing to fear.

Branches chime softly, a tappy beat,
While ants march on, with rhythm so sweet.
They wear tiny shoes, ain't that a treat?
In this concert of critters, they can't be beat.

A bear spins round, in a quirky spin,
With honeyed dreams, he can't help but grin.
The trees shake their leaves, a mischievous kin,
As the forest's laughter is ready to begin.

So listen intently, join in the fun,
When the forest sings, it's never done.
With critters and branches, let's all run,
In this silent song, we're all one.

Vibrations of the Verdant Night

Under starlit skies, the bushes glow,
The crickets chirp in a lively show.
With a hop and a skip, they're stealing the flow,
In this verdant night, let giggles grow.

The owls do hoot, with their silly hats,
While hedgehogs roll, with flumps and splats.
The moon joins in, it's had enough chats,
In the dance of the night, reveal the spats.

Fireflies flicker, a twinkling sight,
Creating a spark in the soft twilight.
They dart and they dash, like sprightly sprites,
In the vibrations of night, we find our delights.

So come take a spin, let your heart ignite,
In this woodland rave, everything feels right.
With laughter galore, oh, what a sight,
In the verdant night, let's dance till daylight.

The Song of the Old Stumps

In a circle of old stumps, we gather around,
Telling tales of the squirrels in leaps that astound.
With acorns as drums, we all start to tap,
While the owls hoot a tune, we all take a nap.

The wind joins the chorus, a mischievous breeze,
Tickling the branches and disturbing the peas.
A raccoon in a top hat jigs with delight,
While the frogs croak a chorus, all snug for the night.

With whispers of laughter, the trees lean in tight,
As we dance with the shadows, what a whimsical sight.
The beetles are buzzin', the fireflies glow,
In this stump-side cabaret, it's a real show!

So raise up your branches, turn up the fun,
For even the squirrels know how to run!
The old stumps are singing, a joyful old throng,
In a forest of giggles, we all sing along.

Echoing the Spirit of the Woods

In the woods there's a giggle, a tickle in the air,
As the rabbits do hop like they just don't care.
The fox holds a concert, his tail is a flag,
With a trumpet made of mushrooms, he's ready to brag.

A rogue band of hedgehogs with instruments fine,
Strike up a tune on thorns and on twine.
The toads join the rhythm; they croak out of time,
While the trees sway in laughter, keeping the rhyme.

The deer form a line, with their hooves on the floor,
And the chipmunks are cheering, always wanting more.
"Encore!" cries the raccoon, with a slap of his paw,
While the badgers keep beat, oh, what a wild draw!

So listen, dear friend, to the chuckles and roars,
In the woods where the spirit of laughter restores.
With every rustle and giggle in the night,
The woods share their echoes, a marvelous sight!

A Chant for the Canopied Retreat

Up above, the branches weave a blanket of green,
Where squirrels conspire, playing pranks that are seen.
The sun peeks through leaves; it's a spotlight of glee,
As the critters all gather for a grand jubilee.

The chipmunk's a bard, with a tall tale to tell,
Of the time that he wrestled a very large shell.
The raccoons all chime in with laughter and cheer,
Creating a chorus that's not quite sincere.

"Let's dance on the branches!" the owl hoots in jest,
With a wink of his eye, he'll throw quite the fest.
The insects hum bass as the frogs jump for grace,
In this canopy party, there's always a space.

So if you find yourself wandering one day,
Lift your eyes to the branches; don't just walk away.
Join in the merriment, let your heart take flight,
In this chant of the trees, from the morning to night!

The Quietude of the Forest Symphony

In a quiet glen echoes a laughter so sweet,
Where pine trees sway gently, tapping their feet.
The crickets compose with a rhythm so rare,
As the hedgehogs gather, all ready to share.

With the bashful old owl offering wisdom and cheer,
The wind blows a melody that all can hear.
The mushrooms stand tall like a chorus of spry,
While the sun filters down like a wink from the sky.

A naughty old squirrel plays tricks in the grass,
With a flick of his tail, he creates quite the sass.
The fox throws a pose, like he's part of the act,
As the forest enlivens, its spirit intact.

So hush now, dear friend, take a seat on the ground,
Let the forest serenade you, with joy all around.
In this quietude, find a symphony's grace,
Where laughter and nature are shared in one space.

Songs of the Whispering Wood

In the woods where the critters play,
A squirrel sings in a clumsy way.
It dances on branches, a comic sight,
While trees laugh softly at its flight.

The porcupine plays the old guitar,
But his quills poke holes, a bizarre star.
With every strum, the owls hoot loud,
Announcing the fun to every crowd.

The rabbits join in with a soft hum,
As the fox taps paws, creating some drum.
This woodland band is quite the show,
Each animal's talent begins to grow.

When twilight falls and shadows creep,
The nighttime symphony makes us leap.
With giggles and snickers, oh what a spree,
In the woods where the laughter runs free!

Beneath the Canopy's Embrace

Beneath the branches, a party's begun,
With fireflies flashing, it's all in fun.
A turtleneck tortoise spins like a top,
While the party-loving raccoon won't stop.

The frogs hold a contest, who can croak best,
And the winning note just brings more jest.
A butterfly's wiggle is quite the dance,
As the wise old owl gives a sidelong glance.

When the acorns fall, they bounce like balls,
Causing giggles and raucous calls.
The chipmunks cheer and take their stance,
Amidst all the laughter, they join in the trance.

As dusk approaches and laughter fades,
The stars giggle in their twinkly parades.
While creatures of night prepare to delight,
A new song begins in the soft moonlight!

Echoes of the Forest Floor

Where the leaves rustle and secrets sneer,
The mushrooms chuckle, 'Come over here!'
With silly faces, they boast and brag,
A squashy little group in a leafy rag.

A hedgehog winks with a side of sass,
'Can you keep up or will you pass?'
They hop and roll in a joyful spree,
While the ants cheer loud from the bumblebee.

Squirrel drops acorns like a clumsy ace,
While hedgehogs race in a nutty chase.
The ruckus blends with the wind's sweet tune,
As shadows dance beneath the moon.

When darkness wraps the forest tight,
The giggles of critters fill up the night.
Echoes of joy bounce far and wide,
Making memories all creatures abide!

A Tapestry of Twigs and Leaves

In a meadow stitched with twigs and leaves,
A party sprouts where everyone believes.
A worm busts moves, the ground shakes fine,
While a snail slides close, sipping sweet brine.

The grasshoppers drum on acorns now,
A toe-tapping tune, oh take a bow!
With each little jump, the butterflies sway,
Spreading joy in a colorful way.

A bear with a hat grins wide with glee,
Sipping on honey from a tall old tree.
While chicks in a chorus chirp and cheer,
Bringing every critter closer near.

As starlit wishes fill the cool air,
Laughter and songs, no room for despair.
In the big forest, under moonbeam's weave,
All friends gather, so happy to believe!

Rhythms of the Rustic Path

On a path of pine and dirt,
A rabbit wears a tiny skirt,
He twirls and hops, what joy, oh fun,
The dance begins beneath the sun.

A squirrel chimes in, oh what a sight,
With acorns flying, it's pure delight,
He spins and flips with cheeky flair,
While birds all laugh without a care.

The lilies laugh, they start to bloom,
As frogs join in with a funny croon,
They pluck their strings, a ribbit song,
Nature's band, where all belong.

As twilight falls, the giggles grow,
In this merry place, the laughter flows,
They share their tales, the night takes flight,
In the rhythms of the path, all feels right.

Cantata of the Quiet Clearing

In a clearing where the daisies sway,
A tortoise struts and leads the way,
With a hat so grand, he steals the show,
Stomping slow, but with great gusto.

The owl nearby, in glasses sits,
With a book of jokes and clever wits,
He hoots and hollers, shares a pun,
As crickets join, the laughs weigh a ton.

A raccoon plays on an old banjo,
With notes so funny, they make hearts glow,
And fireflies dance, like stars they gleam,
Creating a serenade, a nighttime dream.

As moonlight wraps the trees in grace,
The critters dance in a merry race,
In this clearing, joy's song is clear,
The cantata sings for all to hear.

The Arbor's Enchanted Tune

In the shadow of the ancient oak,
A frog sings loud, what a funny poke,
His voice a wibble, his tongue a flap,
As mice applaud, caught in his rap.

The branches sway with a gentle sway,
While chipmunks tap dance in bright array,
With every step, they giggle and squeak,
As butterflies join, waving their streaks.

The wind adds flair, a breeze so kind,
It rustles leaves, a chorus aligned,
A symphony blooms in the sunny glow,
Of laughter shared, and joy does flow.

As dusk approaches, they hum a tune,
Under the watchful eye of the moon,
The magic lingers, delightful and sweet,
In the arbor's arms, they sway to the beat.

Symphony in the Sunlight

With sunlight pouring, the garden gleams,
A hedgehog spins in ridiculous dreams,
With twirls and flips, he steals the scene,
While flowers giggle, all fresh and green.

A bumblebee buzzing, all carefree,
Plays catch with a ladybug, oh what glee,
They race around, a comical chase,
In this vibrant, sunny embrace.

A whacky bear in shades so wide,
Sips lemonade, with joy as his guide,
He clinks his glass, a toast to cheer,
To friendships that bloom throughout the year.

As shadows stretch to bid goodbye,
The garden hums a sweet lullaby,
In the symphony of laughter and light,
Every creature dances, all feels right.

Harmonies in the Heartwood

In the heart of the woods, a squirrel sings,
Bouncing on branches, with acorn bling.
Birds join in with chirps so sweet,
Raccoons tap dance on their furry feet.

A rabbit conducts with a wobbly ear,
While the frogs croak loud, they have no fear.
A turtle's cello makes everyone laugh,
As the fireflies twinkle, they want autographs.

The bumblebees buzz in perfect time,
Creating tunes that are simply sublime.
Even the trees sway to the beat,
With roots that dance, oh, what a treat!

So join this concert, it's a merry sight,
With woodland critters jamming all night.
Harmony flows like a playful stream,
In heartwood's laughter, we gleefully dream.

The Wind's Gentle Composition

Whispers of wind create a soft tune,
As leaves start to shimmy beneath the moon.
A gust sends a pine cone rolling away,
While laughter erupts from the branches at play.

A raccoon in shades tries to rap with flair,
While the owl swoops in, feigning to care.
Grasshoppers strum on a long blade of green,
Making music as wild as they've ever seen.

A deer adds a solo, a soft little hum,
Interrupting the rhythm with a playful thrum.
The chorus of crickets all pitch in loud,
Claiming their rights, they are solemnly proud.

With each rustle and flap, they create a show,
For the moon and the stars, it's a grand, wild flow.
In the calm of the night, the woodland's alive,
With the wind's composition, we joyfully thrive.

Woodland Choirs at Dusk

As the sun dips low and the shadows grow long,
The woodland choir starts their evening song.
Chippers and chortles fill the air,
With a bevy of critters from here and from there.

A hedgehog taps with a thimble-sized drum,
While a fox with a flute makes the melodies hum.
Even the skunks join in with their scent,
Creating a mix that's quite accidental but meant.

The beavers bring wood for a crackling beat,
With snaps and claps, their rhythm's a treat.
Moonlit petals dance in the breeze,
A flower's soft giggle floats 'round with ease.

With every note sung beneath the dark sky,
Giggles and snickers give wings to the shy.
So when dusk falls down and the stars start to gleam,
Woodland choirs gather for a laugh-fueled dream.

Chords of the Misty Dawn

At dawn's first light, the mushrooms convene,
In their curvy caps, a joyous scene.
The fog gives a nod, begins to sway,
While crickets hush and ants start to play.

A crow hoots loudly to set the mood bright,
As the sun peeks in with a beam of delight.
A weasel strums on a twig like a pro,
With notes that dance like a breezy flow.

Even the daisies sway left and right,
In harmony, they feel quite polite.
The grass whispers softly, "What a sweet sound!"
As laughter erupts from the damp, green ground.

In this misty morning, with laughter so loud,
Nature's the star, and all are so proud.
In a jig and a jiggle, the dawn breaks anew,
With chords of delight, it's a whimsical view!

www.ingramcontent.com/pod-product-compliance
Lightning Source LLC
Chambersburg PA
CBHW051640160426
43209CB00004B/732